Disappearance of Skyjacker D. B. Cooper

by Carol Kim

CAPSTONE PRESS
a capstone imprint

Published by Capstone Press, an imprint of Capstone
1710 Roe Crest Drive, North Mankato, Minnesota 56003
capstonepub.com

Copyright © 2022 by Capstone. All rights reserved. No part of this publication may be reproduced in whole or in part, or stored in a retrieval system, or transmitted in any form or by any means, electronic, mechanical, photocopying, recording, or otherwise, without written permission of the publisher.

Library of Congress Cataloging-in-Publication Data
Names: Kim, Carol, author.
Title: Disappearance of skyjacker D.B. Cooper / by Carol Kim.
Description: North Mankato, Minnesota : Capstone Press, [2022] | Series: History's mysteries | Includes bibliographical references and index. | Summary: "On November 24, 1971, a man boarded a passenger plane in Portland, Oregon. Later, he would become known as D. B. Cooper. But that wasn't his real name, and he was no ordinary passenger. He hijacked the plane, demanded $200,000, and parachuted out of the plane with the money. He was never seen again. Who was D. B. Cooper, and what happened to him? Explore the theories behind this crime and why it has become one of history's greatest mysteries"-- Provided by publisher.
Identifiers: LCCN 2021028867 (print) | LCCN 2021028868 (ebook) | ISBN 9781663958761 (hardcover) | ISBN 9781666320718 (paperback) | ISBN 9781666320725 (pdf) | ISBN 9781666320749 (kindle edition)
Subjects: LCSH: Hijacking of aircraft--United States--Case studies--Juvenile literature. | Cooper, D.B.--Juvenile literature.
Classification: LCC HE9803.Z7.H5 K55 2022 (print) | LCC HE9803.Z7.H5 (ebook) | DDC 364.15/520973--dc23
LC record available at https://lccn.loc.gov/2021028867
LC ebook record available at https://lccn.loc.gov/2021028868

Editorial Credits
Editor: Carrie Sheely; Designer: Kim Pfeffer; Media Researcher: Morgan Walters; Production Specialist: Laura Manthe

Image Credits
Alamy: American Photo Archive, 6, JLBvdWOLFe, 14; Associated Press: ASSOCIATED PRESS, top 11, 25, Sue Ogrocki, 27; Getty Images: Bettmann, 8, top 17, bottom 19, somethingway, 15; Newscom: Polaris, bottom 17, top 19; Shutterstock: aapsky, bottom 5, Ekaterina Kondratova, 20, Elizaveta Galitckaia, 21, Milkovasa, 9, Motortion Films, 28, Pressmaster, 7, Salienko Evgenii, 13, sit, Cover, top 5, StockEU, 23; Wikimedia: Tank67, bottom 11

Source Notes
Page 7, "Miss, I have a bomb . . ." "FBI Records: The Vault: D. B. Cooper," Federal Bureau of Investigation, November 30, 1971, file:///Users/csheely/Downloads/D.%20B.%20Cooper%20Part%2008.pdf (Page 17)
Page 13, "No experienced parachutist . . ." "D.B. Cooper Redux," Federal Bureau of Investigation, December 31, 2007, https://archives.fbi.gov/archives/news/stories/2007/december/dbcooper_123107
Page 22, "Could have been . . ." "D.B. Cooper Letter, Newly Released by FBI, Offers Startling Coded Clue That Might Reveal Skyjacker," The Oregonian, January 4, 2018, https://www.oregonlive.com/history/2018/01/db_cooper_letter_recently_rele.html
Page 24, "I'm Dan Cooper" "D.B. Cooper — Found At Last?," CBS News, August 22, 2000, https://www.cbsnews.com/news/d-b-cooper-found-at-last/
Page 26, "My uncle L.D. . . ." Katharine Q. Seelye, "Woman Says Her Uncle Was a Famous Hijacker," The New York Times, August 3, 2011, https://www.nytimes.com/2011/08/04/us/04cooper.html?searchResultPosition=1
Page 26, "We did it . . . " Jonsson, Patrik, "Is 'Uncle L.D.' the notorious skyjacker D.B. Cooper? Experts are skeptical." Christian Science Monitor, 8/4/2011, https://www.csmonitor.com/USA/Justice/2011/0804/Is-Uncle-L.D.-the-notorious-skyjacker-D.B.-Cooper-Experts-are-skeptical

All internet sites appearing in back matter were available and accurate when this book was sent to press.

Table of Contents

Words in **bold** are in the glossary.

INTRODUCTION

A Daring Jump

A man stands on the rear steps of a Boeing 727 airplane. Rain and winds whipping at 200 miles (322 kilometers) per hour are all around him. The plane is flying at an **altitude** of 10,000 feet (3,048 meters). It is somewhere between Seattle, Washington, and Reno, Nevada. With a parachute on his back and $200,000 in cash strapped to his body, the man jumps into the freezing, dark night. He is never seen again.

The man, now known as D. B. Cooper, had **hijacked** the plane and demanded the money. Did he live and get away or did he die?

No one knows if Cooper lived or died after parachuting out of the plane.

The weather was rainy the night Cooper jumped out of the passenger plane.

CHAPTER 1

A Mysterious Passenger with a Criminal Plan

On November 24, 1971, a man who gave his name as Dan Cooper walked up to the Northwest Orient ticket counter at the international airport in Portland, Oregon. He looked like an ordinary businessman. He was around 40 years old. He wore a suit and tie, an overcoat, and dress shoes. He carried a briefcase. The man purchased a ticket to Seattle, Washington.

The Northwest Orient airline ticket for Dan Cooper

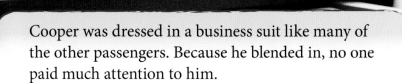

Cooper was dressed in a business suit like many of the other passengers. Because he blended in, no one paid much attention to him.

Cooper took his seat in the back of the aircraft. He soon handed flight attendant Flo Schaffner an envelope. She didn't read it right away. But the man continued to look at her. She felt he wanted her to open it, so she did. There was a note inside the envelope. It read, "Miss, I have a bomb here and I would like you to sit by me."

THE NAME THAT STUCK

Reporter James Long said he wrote one of the first reports on the Cooper plane hijacking. He said he mistakenly reported the hijacker's name was D. B. Cooper. He said there was either a mistake by his source or a bad phone connection. Other reporters then got the story, and continued to use the name of D. B. Cooper. It has stuck ever since!

The Demands

Schaffner sat next to him. Cooper told Schaffner what he wanted: $200,000 in cash, four parachutes, and a refueling truck when they landed.

Schaffner got the note to Tina Mucklow, another flight attendant. Mucklow quickly called the pilots to tell them the plane was being hijacked.

Flo Schaffner talks to reporters after the 1971 hijacking.

After landing, Cooper allowed all the other passengers to leave. Remaining were the two pilots, a flight engineer, and Mucklow. Cooper told the pilots to fly to Mexico City at an altitude no higher than 10,000 feet (3,048 m) and at low speed. He had Mucklow tell him how to lower the plane's rear stairs. Then he told her to join the crew in the cockpit.

Fact

In the 1970s, it was much easier to hijack a plane. Unlike today, passengers did not have to prove who they were. There also were no metal detectors or X-ray machines to help check that dangerous items were not being brought aboard.

Today, luggage goes through a scanner and people walk through a metal detector to help ensure no dangerous items are carried on planes.

The Jump

About 30 to 45 minutes after leaving Seattle, the pilots noticed the rear stair light on the control panel come on. A few minutes later, they felt a dip in the plane. What was happening?

They continued on to Reno, Nevada, so the plane could refuel. As they prepared to land, Mucklow called back to Cooper. She asked him to put up the stairs. There was no answer.

After landing, the crew checked the plane. Cooper, the money, the briefcase, and two parachutes were gone.

What happened to Cooper after he jumped? Could he have survived?

The Boeing 727 that Cooper jumped from on a runway

Fact

In 1972, the Federal Aviation Administration required all aircraft with rear stairs be fitted with a device so they could not be lowered during flight. This locking device is called a Cooper vane.

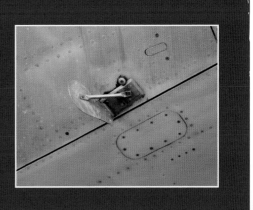

CHAPTER 2

Slim Chance of Survival

Federal Bureau of Investigation (FBI) agents believed Cooper would have had to have been an experienced skydiver to survive such a dangerous jump. Most skydivers jump out of planes flying slower than 100 miles (161 km) per hour. The plane was flying at almost 200 miles (322 km) per hour. At this speed, it is likely a skydiver would quickly start tumbling uncontrollably. The agents thought only someone who had jumped before would know how to regain control. The dark and rainy conditions added to the danger. It would have been hard to see where the ground was and know when to release the parachute.

Dark, stormy weather conditions can make parachute jumps very dangerous.

The **evidence** suggested Cooper was not an expert skydiver. "No experienced parachutist would have jumped in the pitch-black night, in the rain, with a 200-mile-an-hour wind in his face, wearing loafers and a trench coat. . . . ," FBI Special Agent Larry Carr said in 2007.

Of the four parachutes given to him, Cooper chose to use the NB6 military training chute. He failed to see that the reserve chute he took was sewn shut. The military parachute could not be steered. Authorities concluded Cooper would have chosen one of the other chutes if he was a skydiving expert.

The U.S. military has used many kinds of parachutes for training since the 1940s.

Cooper would not have been dressed to survive for a long period of time in the woods.

Agent Carr believes Cooper wouldn't have been able to stop tumbling. As a result, he failed to open his chute. Cooper would have been killed when he hit the ground. Even if he had landed safely, Cooper was not prepared to survive the cold, rainy weather in a heavily wooded area. Wearing business clothes and loafers, he was not dressed for survival. He would have been cold, wet, and possibly injured. He could have died from **hypothermia**.

But why has no body ever been found? Searchers focused on an area covering about 800 square miles (2,000 square kilometers). Finding a body within such a large area would be difficult. Over time, his body would have broken down.

A Mysterious Discovery

In 1980, a boy dug up $5,800 in rotting $20 bills from the banks of the Columbia River in Tena Bar, Washington. It was about 20 miles (32 km) from where Cooper was thought to have landed. The serial numbers matched those of the money Cooper had.

Some investigators believe Cooper may have landed in the Washougal River and drowned. The bills could have washed into the Columbia River and then to Tena Bar. This is known as the Washougal washdown theory.

No other bills ever turned up. Could they all be lost at the bottom of the river, along with Cooper's body?

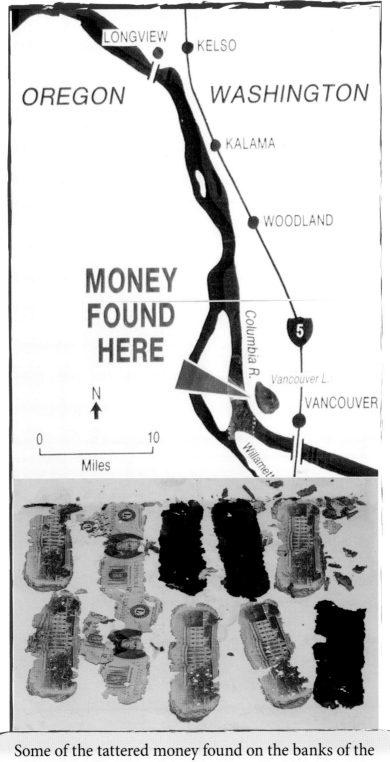

Some of the tattered money found on the banks of the Columbia River

CHAPTER 3

Was Survival Possible?

What Cooper did was very risky. But many people think it is possible he survived. His body was never found. Former FBI agent Richard Tosaw spent thousands of dollars to search the Columbia River in 2005. He hoped to find Cooper's remains. He came up empty-handed.

No other items Cooper took on the jump were ever found. Cooper's parachutes, briefcase, and the rest of the money remain lost. He may have hidden or gotten rid of the evidence after safely landing.

Cooper might have had skydiving experience. He knew how to put on the NB6 parachute. This suggested he had been in the military. Some expert skydivers believe Cooper could have survived even with little skydiving experience.

Fact

Cooper left his necktie behind on the plane. Investigators have used it to collect **DNA** evidence.

The necktie left behind by Cooper

FBI agents dug near the Columbia River to look for more money or evidence after the first bills were found.

Was Cooper Picked Up?

If he landed safely, it is possible Cooper hiked someplace where he could call someone to pick him up. A musician named Jeff Osiadacz was dining at a café near Tena Bar on November 24, 1971. He said he remembered a man coming into the café. The man was soaked from the rain and limping. He asked Osiadacz to give him directions to the café, so he could have a friend pick him up. Could the man have been Cooper?

Some people think Cooper might have called someone to come pick him up in a car after landing safely.

Follow the Money

It is still a mystery how some of the money ended up so far from where Cooper was believed to have landed. If Cooper survived, he could have placed the bills in the river long after the hijacking. Why? Some believe he could have wanted the FBI to think he had drowned. Then they would stop looking for him.

THE TINIEST CLUE

In 2020, Tom Kaye studied the money under a microscope. He found the tiny **algae** on the bills were the kind that bloomed only in the spring. He didn't find the kind of algae that bloom in November on the bills. Kaye believes this proves the money was not in the water right after the jump or for a full year. The finding leaves people to wonder if the money was placed in the river on purpose.

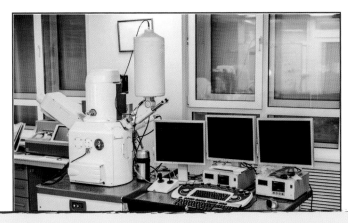

Tom Kaye used an electron microscope to study the algae.

CHAPTER 4

The Suspects

Besides the mystery of whether Cooper lived or died, another question remains: who was Cooper? By 2011, the FBI had looked at more than 1,000 **suspects**. None were proven to be the hijacker. But over the years, police did have some top suspects.

Robert Rackstraw

Letters signed by Cooper were sent to the FBI after the hijacking. A group of investigators said they had decoded hidden messages in the letters. They said one line read, "I am 1st Lt. Robert Rackstraw." A former U.S. Army **paratrooper**, Rackstraw was 28 in 1971. Investigators think he may have worn a **toupee** and makeup. When a reporter once asked Rackstraw if he was Cooper, he replied, "Could have been. Could have been. . . ."

Paratroopers are trained to make safe jumps from planes.

Duane Weber

Duane Weber lay on his deathbed in 1995. He told his wife, Jo Weber, "I'm Dan Cooper." He also said he couldn't remember where he had buried $173,000. Jo later recalled Weber telling her his knee injury was from jumping out of a plane. He had served in the army and he matched the description of Cooper. But a DNA sample from him did not match with the DNA left behind on Cooper's tie.

Richard Floyd McCoy Jr.

Less than five months after the Cooper hijacking, Richard Floyd McCoy Jr. hijacked a 727. He demanded four parachutes and $500,000. He was considered a top suspect because his actions were so similar to Cooper's. But McCoy was ruled out.

Richard Floyd McCoy Jr. was arrested for hijacking a Boeing 727 in April 1972.

Lynn Doyle Cooper

In 2011, the FBI followed another lead in the case. The night before Thanksgiving in 1971, Marla Cooper said her uncle Lynn Doyle (L. D.) and another uncle went turkey hunting. When they returned the next morning, she recalled, "My uncle L. D. was wearing a white T-shirt, and he was bloody and bruised and a mess, and I was horrified. . . . " Later, she overheard him saying, "We did it. Our money problems are over. We hijacked an airplane." Investigators tested a family member's DNA sample to see if it was a partial match to DNA left behind on the tie. But the test came up negative.

Marla Cooper posed with a photograph of her uncle Lynn Doyle Cooper in 2011.

Enduring Mystery

The FBI closed the investigation on D. B. Cooper in 2016. It remains the only unsolved airplane hijacking case. To this day, people remain fascinated with Cooper. There have been books, songs, movies, and even an annual festival inspired by the hijacker. Will we ever know what happened to D. B. Cooper? Did he die, or did he survive and manage to keep his crime a secret? Will we ever know who D. B. Cooper really was? What do you think?

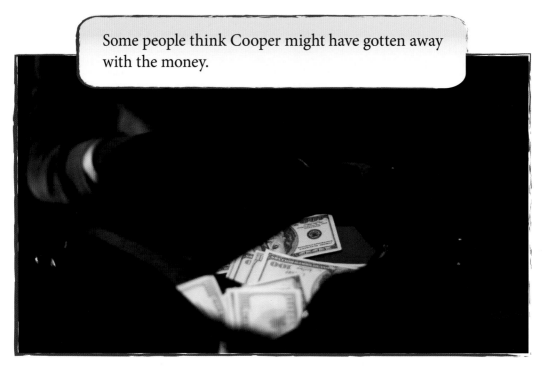

Some people think Cooper might have gotten away with the money.

The Main Theories

1. Cooper did not survive.

The conditions the night Cooper jumped were very dangerous. He may not have been a skilled jumper, and the parachute he chose was not steerable. Cooper was not dressed to survive the cold and wet weather. The only money found was on the banks of the Columbia River. Some people believe it got there because Cooper also ended up in the river and died. The lead FBI agents working on the case believe this theory is the most likely.

2. He survived and was never a suspect.

Other people have hijacked airplanes and survived after parachuting out of them. Cooper could have gained some jumping experience if he was in the military. Cooper could have hidden or destroyed the evidence after surviving the jump. Some people think his identity remains a mystery and that he isn't one of the suspects already named over the years.

3. He survived and is one of the suspects.

The FBI seriously considered many suspects. But without a fingerprint or DNA match, it is hard to prove someone is guilty. The police can't say for sure the DNA on the necktie is from Cooper. They haven't yet made a match to any fingerprints found on the hijacked plane.

Glossary

algae (AL-jee)—small organisms that live in wet places and get their energy from the sun

altitude (AL-ti-tood)—the height of something above ground or above sea level

DNA (dee-en-AY)—material in cells that gives people their individual characteristics; DNA stands for deoxyribonucleic acid

evidence (EV-uh-duhnss)—information, items, and facts that help prove something to be true or false

hijack (HYE-jak)—to take illegal control of a vehicle

hypothermia (hye-puh-THUR-mee-uh)—a condition in which the body temperature falls to dangerously low levels

paratrooper (PAIR-uh-troop-ur)—a soldier trained to jump by parachute into battle

suspect (SUHSS-pekt)—someone who may be responsible for a crime

toupee (tu-PAY)—a wig or section of hair worn to cover a bald spot

Read More

Streissguth, Thomas. *Investigating the D. B. Cooper Hijacking.* New York: AV2 by Weigl, 2020.

Sullivan, Tom. *Unsolved Case Files: Escape at 10,000 Feet: D. B. Cooper and the Missing Money.* New York: Balzar + Bray, 2021.

Walker, Kevin. *Mysterious Disappearances.* Vero Beach, FL: Rourke Educational Media, 2019.

Internet Sites

CitizenSleuths.com: The Hunt for D. B. Cooper
citizensleuths.com/

FBI: D. B. Cooper Hijacking
fbi.gov/history/famous-cases/db-cooper-hijacking

The Last Master Outlaw: How a Team Led by Former FBI Identified Hijacker "D. B. Cooper"
dbcooper.com

Index

Author Biography

Carol Kim is the author of several fiction and nonfiction books for kids. She enjoys researching and uncovering little-known facts and sharing what she learns with young readers. Carol lives in Austin, Texas, with her family. Learn more about her and her latest books at her website, CarolKimBooks.com.